PHONICS CHAPTER BOOKS

The Puppet Club

by Mike Thaler
and Janelle Cherrington
Illustrated by Ana López Escrivá

Scholastic Inc.
New York   Toronto   London   Auckland   Sydney

Copyright © 1998 by Scholastic Inc.
Scholastic *Phonics Chapter Books* is a trademark of Scholastic Inc.
All rights reserved. Published by Scholastic Inc.
Printed in the U.S.A.
ISBN 0-590-11661-4
4 5 6 7 8 9 10   14   04 03 02 01 00 99 98

Dear Teacher/Family Member,

R esearch has shown that phonics is an essential strategy for figuring out unknown words. Early readers need the opportunity to learn letter sounds and how to blend or put them together to make words. These skills must be practiced over and over again by reading stories containing words with the sounds being taught.

T hat's why I'm happy to be an author and Program Coordinator of the **Phonics Chapter Books**. These books provide early readers with playful, fanciful stories in easy-to-manage chapters. More importantly, the words in the stories are controlled for phonics sounds and common sight words. Once sounds and sight words have been introduced, they are continually reviewed and applied in succeeding stories, so children will be able to decode these books—and read them on their own. There is nothing more powerful and encouraging than success.

John Shefelbine
Associate Professor, Reading Education
California State University, Sacramento

CONTENTS

Chapter	Page

1 Jane and Jake

This is a tale about Jane and her little brother, Jake. Jane and Jake like to tell jokes.

One time a big gift box came for them. It had puppets in it, and it had a kit to make a big puppet stage.

"Look at these nice puppets, Jane! I see a dog, a cat, a pig, and a bug. I like the bug," said Jake.

"But what will we do with this big thing, Jake?" Jane asked.

"We can write a play," said Jake. "Then we can do a puppet show. I have a pen."

Jane said, "OK. Write <u>The Race</u>."

As she spoke, Jane got the pig and cat puppets.

"Hmm," she said. "A pig, a cat, a dog, and a bug. Let me think."

Jake said, "The pig says something about having a race. The one who comes in last wins."

"Yes. That's nice, Jake! Then the pig says 1, 2, 3, STOP!" said Jane.

Jake and Jane kept at it until they had a script.

The Race

by Jane and Jake

Pig: Let's have a race. The one who comes in last wins. 1, 2, 3, STOP!

(They all sit.)

Dog: The sun is hot.

Cat: Let's sit in the shade.

Bug: Let's have some cake.

Dog: It is late.

Cat: Let's take a nap.

Pig: We all win the race.
        We all come in last!

"I like that," Jane said. "This is fun."

"I think so, too," said Jake. "Let's make
the stage and show Mom and Dad.
We can see if they like it."

2 A Good Team

Jane and Jake made the stage and let Mom read the script. She said she liked it a lot. So did Jake's friend Mike.

"I think I have some puppets," Mike said. "Can I help with the show?"

Jane said yes, so Mike went home to get his puppets. He had a sheep and a bird.

"Nice puppets," said Jake.

Mike was good with jokes, too. This time the three of them made up the script.

When a Sheep Can't Sleep
by Mike, Jake, and Jane

Sheep: Dog, I can't sleep.

Dog: Take a seat and read.

Sheep: Cat, I can't sleep.

Cat: So eat a meal.

Sheep: I need to sleep, Bird.

Bird: Go sit in a tree.

Sheep: I can't sleep, Pig.

Pig: Keep your feet in some mud.

Sheep: I can't sleep, Bug.

Bug: Well I can, so leave me alone.

Dog: What do you do if you can't
sleep, Sheep?

Sheep: I count my friends.

One, two, three . . .

(Sheep sleeps.)

All: He can count on us!

(They all go to sleep.)

"That's neat!" said Mike. "We could make a good team!"

3 A Breeze

"I like these scripts," said Jake. "Let's write what happens next."

"OK," said Jane. "They all go to sleep. Then what?"

As Jane said this, her friend Beth came. "They dream," Beth said. "You go to sleep and then you dream."

"Yes!" said Mike. "They all dream!"

"Nice work, Beth. That was a big help," Jake said.

"So what is all this?" asked Beth.

Jane said, "We write scripts for puppet shows!"

"I have a frog puppet. Can I help?"
asked Beth.

Jake picked up his pen to write.

Dreams

by Beth, Mike, Jane, and Jake

(Sheep and his friends wake up.)

Sheep: I had a dream!

Pig: What was it about?

Sheep: I was in a tree, and a bee
was on a green leaf.
The bee said, "Be brave
and look at me." I said "No."
And then he bit me!

Bird: In my dream, I WAS a leaf
in a tree.

Dog: In my dream, I had a bone to eat.

Frog: In my dream, I had a drink of fresh iced tea.

Bug: In my dream, I gave a speech.

Sheep: About what?

Bug: About gumdrops and dots.

Cat: I often dream of cream, but I did not have a dream.

Sheep: You can have mine.

Cat: No thanks. You can keep it.

"That was a breeze!" said Beth.

4 Things Click

"It was a piece of cake!" said Jane. "These are good scripts for puppet shows. We work well as a team!"

"Piece of cake," said Jake. "I like it. That's the name of the next script."

Mike said, "No. I think <u>Bake a Cake</u> is good."

"<u>Bake a Cake</u> it is," said Beth.

Bake a Cake

by Jane, Jake, Beth, and Mike

Dog: I have a plan. Let's bake a cake.

Sheep: What would you like
        on the cake, Dog?

Dog: I would like a nice
        clean bone on the cake.

Sheep: What would you like
        on the cake, Cat?

Cat: I would flip for some
        cream on the cake.

Sheep: What would you
        like on the cake, Pig?

Pig: I would like some thick
        black mud on the cake.

Sheep: What would you like
        on the cake, Bug?

Bug: I would like many,
            many blades of grass.

Sheep: What would you like
            on the cake, Frog?

Frog: Could I have a bug
            on the cake?

Bug: I am a bug. That's not nice!

Sheep: Let's blend the mix and
            bake the cake.

21

Pig: When can we have it?

Sheep: When it fluffs up.

Cat: It will be a good cake!

Bug: It will be a big cake!

Dog: It will be a fine cake!

Sheep: At last! It is time to take the cake out!

        (They all clap.)

Pig: Let's all take a big bite.

Dog: But where is Bird?

Cat: He is home.

Sheep: We could save some cake for him, just a little slice.

All: Yes! He eats like a bird.

5 Good Stuff

"This is good stuff!" Mike said. "I think this could be a nice puppet show."

"I think so, too," said Beth. "Can we write a little bit more, so it will be more like a play?"

Just as Beth said that, her friend Steve came. Steve lived just down the block.

"What's up?" Steve asked. "I see puppets, a stage, scripts, and all of you. Is this a puppet club or something?"

"The Puppet Club!" said Jake. "Yes. That's just what this is!"

"Can I help, too?" Steve asked. "It looks like fun. Which puppet can I use?"

The Snake

by The Puppet Club

Sheep: What would you do if
a snake came to steal
some of this cake?

Bug: I would stand up and be
as big as I could.

Cat: I would give the snake some
cake. Then I would go to sleep.

Bird: I would go up in the tree.

Dog: I would get a stick.

Frog: I would get a stone.

Pig: I would make a plan.

Sheep: Then what would you do?

Bug: I would step on it.

Bird: I would snap at it.

Cat: I would still be sleeping.

Dog: I would stand on it.

Frog: I would stomp on it.

Pig: I would spin on it until it was
a spot.

Sheep: Look down. I think I see a snake.

All: We have to leave!

(They all run fast.)

6 What's Next?

Steve said, "We need an ending.
We can't just let them run out like that."

"Let's think for a little while,"
said Jane.

"When they stop, Dog could ask
if the snake chased them," Beth said.

"OK. Let's see if that will work,"
said Mike.

Whistle

by The Puppet Club

(The seven friends have just
run a mile to escape a snake.)

All: Wheeze, wheeze, wheeze!

Dog: Did the snake chase us?

Pig: Check and see.

Sheep: I did. It was not a snake.
It was just a stick.

Cat: Let's go. I need some lunch.

Sheep: We can whistle while we go.

Cat: I can't whistle, but I can whine.

Pig: I can wheeze.

Bird: I can tweet.

Dog: I can whimper.

Bug: I can squeak.

Frog: I can do all those things.
Which one is best?

Sheep: I will teach you to whistle.
Puff out your chests like this.
One, two, three!

All: (At the same time) Whistle!
Whine! Wheeze! Tweet!
Whimper! Squeak! Ribbit!

Sheep: That was nice. It just needs
a little work.

All: We all won a race.
We all had a dream.
We all had some cake.
We all ran from a snake.
And we all can whistle!

Sheep: (With a big smile) Yes!

"That was fun, but I hope it's not
the end of our puppet club," said Beth.

"No," said Mike. "We can meet
all the time."

"We can write more stuff," Jake said.

"We can get more friends to help us,"
said Steve.

"We can even make more puppets,"
Jane said. "This is The Puppet Club!"

PHONICS

Decodable Words With the Phonic Elements

1

a-e	-ace
came	race
Jane	
late	**-ake**
shade	cake
tale	Jake
	make
e-e	take
these	
	-oke
i-e	jokes
like	spoke
time	
	-ice
	nice

2

e	ee
he	feet
she	keep
we	need
	Sheep
ea	sleep
leave	three
meal	tree
read	
team	

-eat
eat
neat
seat

3

r-blends
brave
breeze
cream
dream
drink
fresh
green
tree
gumdrops

4

l-blends
black
blades
blend
clap
clean
click
flip
fluffs
plan
slice

5

s-blends
sleep
snake
snap
spin
spot
stand
steal
step
Steve
stick
still
stomp
stone
stuff
asked
fast
just

6

ch	th
chase	that
check	them
chests	things
lunch	think
teach	this
	three
sh	Beth
Sheep	
	wh
	what's
	wheeze
	when
	which
	while
	whine

Contents

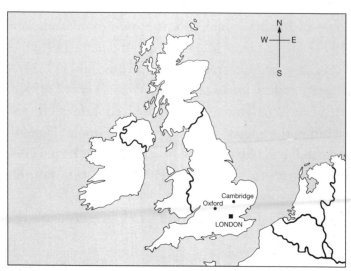

A Note About the Author

M.R. James (Montague Rhodes James) was born on 1st August 1862. His family lived in a small village in Suffolk, in the eastern part of England. James' father worked in a church. He was a clergyman. M.R. James had two brothers and one sister.

M.R. James was very clever. From 1876 to 1882, he was a pupil at Eton. This is a famous school for boys. In 1882, James studied at King's College in Cambridge University.

M.R. James was interested in languages, religion, science and literature. He wrote about architecture. He studied the Bible. He wrote books about many things.

M.R. James also wrote very many ghost stories. Some of his books are: *Ghost Stories of an Antiquary* (1904), *More Ghost Stories of an Antiquary* (1911), *A Thin Ghost and Others* (1919), *The Five Jars* (1922), *A Warning to the Curious and Other Ghost Stories* (1925).

Every Christmas, friends visited James. In the evenings, the guests sat in James' sitting-room. James lit one candle and he put it by his chair. Then he read one of his stories to his friends. The stories were horrible and frightening!

In 1893, James became the Director of the

Fitzwilliam Museum in Cambridge. From 1913, James was Vice-Chancellor of Cambridge University. He worked very hard. Everybody liked him. In 1918 James became Provost of Eton. He loved his job at this school. M.R. James died on 12th June 1936. He was 74 years old.

A Note About These Stories

Times: 1895 and 1859.

Places: Oxford and other places in England.

These two stories were first published in 1904. They were in a book called *Ghost Stories of an Antiquary*. The first story, *The House in the Picture*, was called 'The Mezzotint'. The second story, *Abbot Thomas' Treasure*, was called 'The Treasure of Abbot Thomas'. .

In the 1800s, the money in Britain was pounds (£), shillings (s) and pence (d). £1.1s.0d = 105p today.

M.R. James often wrote stories about gentlemen and scholars. These very intelligent men lived in rooms at the colleges of universities. They studied many subjects and they talked with their friends. Servants looked after the scholars. At this time, men called their friends by their last names, e.g. Mr Williams calls his friend, Mr Garwood, 'Garwood'. But servants were called by their first names.

Note: St = Saint (e.g. St Bega's Abbey). Job, St John and Zechariah, say: dʒeʊb, sənt 'dʒɒn and zekə'raɪə.

THE HOUSE IN THE PICTURE

1

An Old Engraving

J.W. Britnell – Art Dealer

COURTENAY STREET

LONDON SW1

Mr D. Williams
The University Museum
Oxford

10th February 1895

Dear Mr Williams,
Here is our new catalogue. There
are many interesting pictures
in it. Number 97 – on page 45 –
is very interesting. Do you
want to look at this picture?
I can send it to you quickly.

Yours sincerely,

J. W. Britnell

J. W. BRITNELL

It was Thursday morning. Mr Williams was sitting in his office in the Oxford University Museum. Mr Williams was reading the letter from Mr Britnell.

Mr Britnell was an art dealer – he sold pictures. And Mr Williams often bought pictures from Mr Britnell. Mr Williams bought pictures for the museum. He tried to find interesting pictures for the museum – paintings, drawings or engravings. Mr Williams was interested in old pictures of great houses. And he was interested in old pictures of towns and villages in England.

Mr Williams put down the letter. He picked up Mr Britnell's new catalogue and he opened it at page 45. He read about picture number 97.

J.W. Britnell — *Catalogue* — *February 1895*

97.   A very interesting engraving. A picture of a large house with a garden. The date of the house is about 1700.

Artist: The picture is signed by 'A.F.'

Date: 1800?

Price: £12.0s.0d.

45

Mr Williams was surprised.

'This picture is very expensive!' he said to himself. 'I will not pay twelve pounds for an engraving of a house! Why does Britnell want to send this picture to me?'

Then he thought for a moment.

'Britnell is a clever man,' he said to himself. 'He likes this engraving. And I want some more engravings for the museum. I will look at it.'

Mr Williams sent a short letter to Mr Britnell.

D. Williams, M.A.
Canterbury College, Oxford

Mr J. W. Britnell
Courtenay Street
London

11th February 1895

Dear Mr Britnell
Please send Picture Number 97. I will look at this engraving. Please send it to my rooms at Canterbury College. Thank you.

D. Williams

Mr Williams put the letter into an envelope.

'Some artists are very clever,' he said to himself. 'Some artists make beautiful engravings. But many artists are not very clever. And they make very bad engravings! Will this be a good engraving?'

Mr Williams lived in two large rooms at Canterbury College. At one o'clock on Saturday afternoon, he was at home. He was in his sitting-room. He was sitting next to a big fire and he was reading a book.

Somebody knocked on the door. Mr Williams put down his book. He went to the door and he opened it.

'Here is a parcel for you, sir,' said his servant.

'Thank you, James,' said Mr Williams. He took the parcel from the servant and he closed the door. The parcel was from Mr Britnell.

'This has arrived very quickly,' Mr Williams said to himself. 'I'll look at your expensive picture, Britnell. Then I'll send it back to you on Monday!' And he laughed.

Mr Williams opened the parcel and he lifted up the engraving.

'What is this?' he said. And he looked carefully at the picture.

The small engraving showed the front of a large

house. There were three rows of big windows. There was a big door. Next to the house, there were tall trees. And in front of the house, there was a lot of grass – a large lawn. The sky in the picture was very dark. At the bottom of the picture, there were two letters – the initials of the artist – A.F.

'What is this?' Mr Williams said again. 'It is an old picture of a large house in the country. The house was built at the beginning of the eighteenth century. But it is not an interesting house. And it is a bad engraving. The picture shows the house at night. Why has the artist done this? Why did Britnell send the picture to me? And why does he want twelve pounds for it?'

Mr Williams looked at the back of the picture. There was a piece of paper on the back of the frame. There was some writing on this paper, but the left side of the paper was torn. Mr Williams read the ends of some words.

ngley Hall,
ssex,
ngland

Mr Williams put the engraving down on a table. Then he went to a bookshelf. He started to look for a book.

'I have a book called *The Great Houses of England*,' he said to himself. 'Where is it? I don't know. But I must go out now. I'll look for the book later.'

———

At half past four, Mr Williams was at home again. Suddenly, somebody knocked on his door. Mr Williams opened it. A tall, thin man was standing there.

'Hello, Binks,' said Mr Williams.

'Hello, Williams,' said the man. 'Are you working?'

'No, no. Come in. Come in,' said Mr Williams. 'I'm going to have some tea soon.'

Professor Binks was a scientist. He lived in Canterbury College too. He came into the room and he sat at the table.

The sky was dark outside the window. Mr Williams lit the lamps in the room. Then he closed the curtains.

Professor Binks picked up the engraving.

'What's this, Williams?' he asked. 'Are you going to buy it for the museum? How did the artist make it?'

'It's an engraving, Binks,' replied Mr Williams.

11

'Engravings are printed on paper. The artist cuts lines on a piece of metal. He makes his picture with these lines. He puts black ink on the metal. Then he wipes the ink off the metal, but some ink stays in the cuts. Then the artist puts a piece of paper on the metal. He presses on the paper. The picture is printed onto the paper. An artist can make many pictures on paper from the metal picture.'

'That's very clever,' said Professor Binks.

'That artist – A.F. – was not very clever,' said Mr Williams. 'That is a very bad engraving. I'm going to send it back to the art dealer. The picture is very expensive and it isn't very interesting. There are no people in the picture – there are no figures in it. But I want to know something. Where is the house? I have a book called *The Great Houses of England*. I must look for it.'

Mr Williams went back to his bookshelves.

'Look at the back of the picture,' he said to his friend. 'The words are an address. But some letters are gone. Look at the last line of writing. The house is in England. Look at the middle line. The house is in the county of Sussex or the county of Essex. Look at the first line of writing. The house is called *Something*-ley Hall.'

But Professor Binks was not listening to Mr Williams. He was looking at the picture again.

'It's not a *very* bad picture,' he said. 'I like the moon and the moonlight. And there *is* a figure – a person.

There is a figure at the bottom of the picture.'

'Give the picture to me, Binks,' said Mr Williams.

'Yes, the moonlight is good,' he said. 'I didn't see that before. But where is the person? Oh, I see it. There's a head at the bottom of the picture. Is it a man or a woman? I don't know.'

Mr Williams thought for a moment.

'That *is* strange! I didn't see it before,' he said. 'And I didn't see the moonlight.'

The moonlight was there in the picture. And there was a dark shape at the bottom of the engraving. It was the back of somebody's head. The person was wearing a hood.

'You're right,' said Mr Williams. 'It isn't a very bad picture. But it *is* very expensive. I won't buy it.'

Mr Williams' servant knocked on the door and he brought tea for the two men.

Professor Binks and Mr Williams drank their tea together. Then the professor went back to his rooms. Soon, Mr Williams found the book called *The Great Houses of England*. He opened the book. He tried to find the house in the picture.

'This is very difficult,' he said to himself. 'N-G-L-E-Y could be the end of Langley or Guestingley. Or lots of other names! I'll never find the house in this book.'

At seven o'clock he put the book back on the bookshelf. He went out of his rooms. He was going to have his dinner.

He left the engraving on the table.

The House in the Moonlight

After dinner, some of Mr Williams' friends came to his rooms. They sat near the fire and they drank coffee.

One of Mr Williams' friends was called Mr Garwood. Mr Garwood liked pictures. He saw the engraving on Mr Williams' table. He walked over to the table and he looked quickly at the picture. Then he looked at it again. He looked at it very carefully.

'This is a very good picture, Williams,' Mr Garwood said. 'It's a fine engraving! The moonlight is good. And the figure of the person is very good too. It's a strange figure. But the artist has shown it very well.'

'Yes, yes, it's a good picture,' said Mr Williams. He was talking to another friend. He did not listen carefully to Mr Garwood. And he did not look at the engraving.

Two hours later, the visitors had left. Mr Williams picked up a lamp. He went towards his bedroom. The engraving was lying on the table. The light from the lamp shone on it. Mr Williams saw the picture and he stopped suddenly. His hands shook. His face was pale. He was frightened!

Carefully, Mr Williams put the lamp on the table. Carefully, he looked at the picture.

There was a figure in front of the house. But it had changed. It was not at the bottom of the picture. It was on the lawn! It was near the house. The figure was wearing a big black cloak. On the cloak, there was a white circle.

'This is very strange!' Mr Williams said to himself. 'Is the figure walking towards the house?'

Mr Williams picked up the picture. Quickly, he put

it in a big cupboard and he locked the cupboard door.

Next, he went to the table and he sat down. He wrote a few sentences on a piece of paper. Then he put the paper in another cupboard – a smaller cupboard. He locked the door of that cupboard too.

Mr Williams went to bed. But he did not sleep well.

———

Early the next morning, Mr Williams visited his friend, Mr Nisbet. Mr Nisbet lived near Mr Williams.

'Good morning, Nisbet,' said Mr Williams. 'Will you come to my rooms, please? I want to show you something.'

'Are you ill?' asked Mr Nisbet. 'Your face is pale.'

Mr Williams did not answer. He took Mr Nisbet to his rooms. Quickly, he unlocked the door of the big cupboard. He took out the picture. He gave it to his friend. He did not look at the picture himself.

'Tell me about the picture,' said Mr Williams. 'Describe it, please.'

'Why?' asked Mr Nisbet.

'Please describe the picture carefully,' replied Mr Williams. 'Then I will tell you about it.'

'It's an old picture of a large house,' said Mr Nisbet.

Then Mr Nisbet looked at the picture carefully.

'There is moonlight,' he said. 'And there are clouds.'

'There was no moon at first,' said Mr Williams.

'The house has three rows of windows,' said Mr Nisbet. 'There is a door in the middle —'

'Is there a figure – a person?' asked Mr Williams.

'No, there isn't a figure,' replied Mr Nisbet.

'Isn't there a figure on the lawn?' asked Mr Williams.

'No, there isn't a figure on the lawn,' replied his friend. 'But one of the windows near the door is open.'

'A window is open!' shouted Mr Williams. He was very excited. He took the picture from his friend.

Yes! A window *was* open. And there was no figure in the picture!

'It's not on the lawn,' said Mr Williams quietly. 'It's in the house!'

'What is in the house?' asked Mr Nisbet.

'The figure,' replied Mr Williams. 'Please write a description of the picture, Nisbet.' He gave his friend a piece of paper.

Mr Nisbet was surprised. But he sat down and he wrote a description of the picture. Then Mr Williams unlocked the door of the small cupboard. He took a piece of paper from the cupboard and he gave it to Mr Nisbet.

'I wrote this description of the picture at midnight,' Mr Williams said. 'Please read it.'

Mr Nisbet read the description. Then he read his own description again.

'What is happening?' he asked.

'I don't know,' replied Mr Williams. 'But it's a very strange engraving! At one o'clock yesterday afternoon, I looked at the picture. It showed the front of a large house. There was no figure. There was a dark sky. There was no moonlight. There were no clouds. It wasn't a very interesting picture.'

'I don't understand,' said Mr Nisbet.

'Please listen to me, Nisbet,' Mr Williams said. 'Professor Binks saw the picture at half past four. He saw moonlight. He saw clouds. And he saw a figure. He saw the back of somebody's head – here.' Mr Williams pointed to the bottom of the picture.

'At midnight, I looked at the picture again,' said Mr Williams. 'I saw a figure on the lawn, near the house. Its face was towards the house. It was wearing a big black cloak. On the cloak, there was a white circle.'

'I don't understand,' said Mr Nisbet.

'Garwood saw the engraving yesterday evening,' said Mr Williams. 'What did Garwood see then?'

Mr Williams was excited. 'I must speak to Garwood,' he said. He ran out of the room. Very soon, he returned with Mr Garwood. Mr Garwood sat down. He answered Mr Williams' questions.

'The moonlight in the picture was very bright,' Mr Garwood said. 'And the figure was standing in the middle of the lawn. The figure was looking at the house. And it was wearing a black cloak. The hood of the cloak was over the figure's head. I saw the back of the cloak. There was a strange white circle on the cloak.'

The three men looked at each other.

'What is happening?' asked Mr Nisbet.

'We are seeing a terrible story in this picture,' replied Mr Williams. 'I have three questions. Did these things happen in the past? Are these things happening now? Will these things happen in the future? I do not know the answers.'

'What shall we do?' asked Mr Garwood.

'We must find out about the house,' said Mr Williams. 'Let's ask Professor Green. He knows about great English houses.'

'Professor Green is on holiday,' said Mr Nisbet. 'But he'll return to the college tomorrow.'

'Then we'll ask him about the house tomorrow,' said Mr Williams. 'Let's walk to the river now.'

———

At three o'clock, the men returned to Mr Williams' rooms. The door was open. The three friends went in.

Mr Williams' servant was in the sitting-room. He was looking at the picture.

The servant's face was pale. He was frightened.

'I'm sorry, sir,' he said to Mr Williams. 'I was going to clean your rooms. Then I saw this terrible thing!'

The man pointed at the picture. But his hand was shaking.

'I don't like this picture, sir,' he said.

'Are you frightened of a picture, James?' asked Mr Williams.

'It's a terrible picture, sir,' said the servant. 'I looked at it and I saw this black thing. I saw its white bones. It's a skeleton, sir! It's horrible! And then I saw the poor little baby!'

'I'm sorry, sir. I'll go now, sir,' said the frightened servant. And he ran out of the room.

The three men looked at the engraving. They saw the house and they saw the clouds in the sky. They saw the moonlight. But there were no open windows in the house.

The figure was on the lawn again. Was it walking away from the house? The moonlight was shining on the figure. The three men saw the figure's thin, long legs. They saw a small part of its face.

'Look,' said Mr Williams quietly. 'James was right. It is a skeleton!'

'And it's carrying something,' said Mr Garwood. 'What is it carrying?'

'It's carrying a baby or a small child,' replied Mr Nisbet. 'Is the baby dead or alive?'

'I don't know,' said Mr Williams.

For four hours, the men looked at the picture. Nothing happened. Nothing changed. The figure stood on the lawn with the child. But it did not move.

At seven o'clock, the three men went out. They had dinner together. They ate quietly. They did not talk.

After dinner, they went back to Mr Williams' rooms. The engraving was lying on the table. But the figure had gone. The child had gone. There was no moon and there were no clouds. The sky was dark.

'I saw *this* picture at one o'clock yesterday afternoon,' Mr Williams said. 'The story has ended now.'

'Let's try to find the house in one of your books again,' said Mr Nisbet.

The three men looked at many books. They tried to find the house in the picture.

Suddenly, Mr Williams spoke.

'Look at this,' he said. 'Here are the answers to our questions!'

Mr Williams showed his friends a page of a book. The book was called *The Towns and Villages of Essex*.

The Towns and Villages of Essex

Anningley. There are two interesting buildings in this small village. They are the church and Anningley Hall. In the church are the graves of the Francis family and the Gawdy family.

Anningley Hall was built in 1705. It is a large stone house. It has a large garden. Anningley Hall was the home of the Francis family until the early nineteenth century.

In 1798, Arthur Francis got married. Arthur and his wife had one son, George. In 1801, Arthur Francis' wife died. Then, in April 1802, George Francis disappeared from Anningley Hall. He was two years old. Nobody could find the little boy. Arthur Francis, George's father, was the last person in the family. But he died in 1805.

Arthur Francis was an artist. He made many engravings. A week before his death, he made an engraving of his home, Anningley Hall.

[368]

3

Professor Green's Story

The next day, the three men talked to Professor Green. They showed him the strange engraving and they told him their story.

'Yes, this is Anningley Hall,' said Professor Green. 'Long ago, I lived in Essex. I know the house and the village.'

'Please tell us about the house, Professor,' said Mr Williams. 'What happened there?'

'Arthur Francis was a cruel man,' said Professor Green. 'He owned a lot of land near the village of Anningley. There were lots of birds and animals on Arthur Francis' land. Often, people from the village were hungry. They caught and killed the birds and the animals. They ate them.'

'Yes, I understand,' said Mr Garwood. 'The village people were poachers,' said Mr Garwood.

'Yes, that's right,' replied Professor Green. 'And Arthur Francis hated poachers.'

'Many rich men hate poachers,' said Mr Williams.

'Yes,' said the professor. 'But Arthur Francis hated one poacher very much. And the poacher hated him. This man was called Jack Gawdy.'

'Why did Francis hate Gawdy?' asked Mr Garwood.

'And why did Gawdy hate Francis?' asked Mr Nisbet.

'Once, the Gawdy family had been rich and important,' replied Professor Green. 'But they had lost their money. Jack Gawdy was poor and Arthur Francis was rich. Jack was the last person in the Gawdy family. He had no parents and no brothers or sisters. He had no wife and no children.'

'What happened, Professor?' asked Mr Williams.

'One night, Gawdy was poaching birds on Arthur Francis' land,' said Professor Green. 'Gawdy made a terrible mistake. He shot a man – one of Arthur

Francis' servants. The man died – Jack Gawdy was a murderer. In January 1802, Gawdy was hanged. Arthur Francis was happy.'

'But what did we see in the picture?' asked Mr Garwood.

'Listen! I'll tell you!' said Professor Green. 'One night in April 1802, Arthur Francis' young son, George, disappeared. Nobody could find the boy. The people in the village said, "Gawdy's friends took the boy and they killed him. They were angry with Arthur Francis. Jack Gawdy was the last person in the Gawdy family. His friends killed the last person in the Francis family." Everybody in the village told that story. And everybody in the village believed the story.'

'But the story wasn't true,' said Mr Williams. 'We know the truth. Jack Gawdy himself took the child. Gawdy was hanged. He was dead! But he came back and he took the boy. We saw him in the picture!'

The men looked at each other.

'Yes,' said old Professor Green. 'Arthur Francis made that engraving.' He pointed at the picture. 'Those are his initials – A.F.,' he said. 'Now the picture has told you the *true* story.'

ABBOT THOMAS' TREASURE

1

The Archeologist

It was a summer day in 1859. Mr Somerton was sitting in his library. He was reading a book. It was half past four in the afternoon. Mr Somerton had started reading the book at ten o'clock!

Outside, the sun was shining and the sky was blue. It was a beautiful summer day. But Mr Somerton was not interested in the sun and the sky. He was interested in his book.

Mr Somerton was about forty years old and he was a rich man. He lived in a large house in the south of England. He was not married. His servant, George, took care of him.

Mr Somerton was an archeologist. He was interested in old buildings. And he was interested in the remains of old buildings. There were many hundreds of books on the shelves in Mr Somerton's library. All the books were about archeology.

Mr Somerton read about archeology and he wrote about archeology. Sometimes he visited the remains of some old buildings. But often, he sat in his library all day.

The archeologist was reading about old buildings on that day in 1859. On that day, Mr Somerton was a happy man!

———

Somebody knocked on the door of the library.

'Come in!' said Mr Somerton.

George came into the room. He was carrying an envelope.

'This letter has arrived from London, sir,' he said. He gave the envelope to Mr Somerton.

'Thank you, George,' said the archeologist. 'Please bring me some tea in one hour.'

'Yes, sir,' said the servant. Quietly, he left the room.

Mr Somerton quickly opened the envelope. The letter was from a bookseller in London. There was some news in the letter, and it was good news. The archeologist had waited for this news for a long time.

JOSEPH NEWTON
THE LONDON BOOKSHOP

Dear Mr Somerton —   11th August 1859

I have some good news. At last, I have the book! I have 'The History of St Bega's Abbey' for you.

The price is £20.12s.0d. Please send the money to me. I will send the book to your home immediately.

Yours sincerely
Joseph Newton

Joseph Newton

Mr Somerton was very interested in the history of St Bega's Abbey. The archeologist had visited many bookshops in England. For many years, he had tried to find this book. And at last, Mr Newton had found it for him!

The archeologist quickly wrote a note to Mr Newton. He put the note and a cheque for £20.12s.0d in an envelope. He wrote the bookseller's address on the envelope. Then he called his servant.

'George,' he said. 'I don't want any tea. Please take this letter to the post office.'

'Yes, sir,' said George.

The servant took the envelope and he quickly left the room.

Mr Somerton smiled. Then he started to read again.

Two days later, the book arrived from London. George brought it to the library in the afternoon. He gave it to Mr Somerton. It was a very old book. It had a leather cover. The title was on the front of the book. The title was in gold letters.

'At last, I've got it,' said Mr Somerton. 'Thank you, George.'

A few years before, Mr Somerton had heard about the remains of St Bega's Abbey. The remains were in a green field near the small town of St Bega's. The town was in the north of England. The remains were a few small parts of the stone walls of the abbey.

Mr Somerton opened the book and he started to read. He was happy!

2

St Bega's Abbey

Long ago, there were many buildings at St Bega's Abbey. A hundred monks lived there. The monks prayed in the abbey church. They worked in the abbey hospital and they worked in the abbey's fields.

In the sixteenth century, the great abbey church had beautiful new windows. These windows were famous. They were made of beautiful painted glass. The paintings on the windows told stories. The painted windows told stories from the Bible. The monks taught people about the Bible. Many people could not read or write. They learnt the Bible-stories from the painted-glass windows in churches.

The chief monk of an abbey was called the abbot. At the beginning of the sixteenth century, the abbot of St Bega's was a man called Thomas. Abbot Thomas paid for many fine new buildings at the abbey. And he paid for the beautiful painted-glass windows too.

But later in the sixteenth century, there was a very powerful king in England. He did not like the monks. The monks were very rich. They owned a lot of land. The king wanted their money and their land. He took the abbeys away from the monks. He took their money and their land. Then his soldiers destroyed the abbeys.

The soldiers pulled down the great stone churches and they took away the painted glass. Sometimes, they pulled down the monks' stone houses.

The king gave the stones and the glass to his friends. Many of the rich men in England built great houses with the stones. And they put the painted glass into these houses.

Mr Somerton was interested in old painted glass.

'Where is the painted glass from St Bega's Abbey?' the archeologist asked himself. 'I must find out about Abbot Thomas' glass. Will this old book give me some information about Abbot Thomas?'

Soon, the archeologist was reading about Abbot Thomas in his book.

The History of St Bega's Abbey

Abbot Thomas was a very rich man. He paid for the beautiful new painted-glass windows in the abbey church.

Near the abbot's house, there was a very deep well. The monks got water from this well.

Abbot Thomas paid for a beautiful new stone well-head.

There were many strange carvings on the well-head.

'This is interesting,' Mr Somerton said to himself. 'Is the well-head at St Bega's now? The king's soldiers did not destroy wells. People always wanted water.'

Then the archeologist turned the page of his book. He read the next page.

The History of St Bega's Abbey

Abbot Thomas was a very rich man. He did not spend all his money on the abbey. He hid some treasure – thousands of gold coins – in the abbey. He told the other monks about this hidden treasure. But he did not tell them about the hiding-place. The monks often asked him about the hiding-place. He always said, 'Job, John and Zechariah will tell you about it. Or they will tell somebody in the future.'

Abbot Thomas did not tell anybody his secret. He did not tell anybody about the hiding-place. Then he died suddenly. Many monks tried to find the treasure. Later, the king's soldiers tried to find it. But nobody has found Abbot Thomas' treasure.

'Job, John and Zechariah!' Mr Somerton said to himself. 'I remember something about those names.'

He thought for a few minutes. Then he remembered! One day, he had visited the house of Lord Dunstan. Lord Dunstan lived in a beautiful house, in the middle of England. In the Great Hall of this house there were three huge painted-glass windows. And in each window, there was a picture of a person.

The people in these pictures were people from the stories in the Bible. On the left window, there was a picture of the man called Job. The middle window had a picture of St John. And on the right window, there was a picture of Zechariah.

'The artist painted those windows at the beginning of the sixteenth century,' thought the archeologist. 'He painted them in the time of Abbot Thomas. Now I know something else about those windows. They came from St Bega's Abbey!'

'Yes, this is very interesting,' Mr Somerton thought. 'Abbot Thomas said, "Job, John and Zechariah will tell you about the hiding-place." Will they tell *me* about the hiding-place? Will I find the treasure?'

The archeologist wrote a letter to Lord Dunstan.

A few minutes later, George came into the library. He brought Mr Somerton some tea. Mr Somerton gave the letter to his servant.

'Please take this to the post office, George,' he said.

Three days later, Lord Dunstan replied to Mr Somerton's letter. He invited the archeologist to his house.

Mr Somerton called George.

'Please put some clothes in our bags, George,' he said. 'We are going to visit Lord Dunstan tomorrow.'

3

The Three Windows

Two days later, Mr Somerton was standing in the Great Hall of Lord Dunstan's house. George was standing next to him. It was Sunday. And it was a beautiful, sunny morning.

The two men were looking up at three very large painted-glass windows. There was a tall figure painted on the glass of each window. And beneath each figure, Mr Somerton saw the person's name. Each name was in red letters.

'Do you see, George?' said the archeologist. 'The person on the left window is Job. John is on the middle window. John was a saint. And that is Zechariah on the right window.'

'I see the names, sir,' said George. 'But are they three different men? They are all wearing yellow cloaks. Each cloak has a black edge at the bottom. Each man is holding up his right hand. And all the men have beards!'

'That's true, George,' said the archeologist. And he laughed. 'But they are three different men.'

'Look again, George,' Mr Somerton said. 'Each man is holding an open book in his left hand. And there are words on the pages of the books. All the words are from the Bible. Each book has a sentence from a Bible-story. The story is about the man in the picture.'

Mr Somerton read the sentence on Zechariah's book.

'The words on Zechariah's book are, "There are seven eyes on one stone."' he said. 'Yes, yes, that is a sentence from the Bible. It's from the story about Zechariah.'

Then the archeologist read the sentence on Job's book.

'The words on Job's book are, "Gold is hidden in this place."' he said. 'But that isn't right, George! The artist has painted a wrong word on this book. In the Bible, the words are, "Gold is heated in this place." That is strange!'

Mr Somerton looked at the middle window. St John's book had more words than the other books.

'Yes, this is *very* strange, George!' the archeologist said. 'St John's book has two sentences. The words are, "There is writing on their cloaks. Nobody knows about it." The first sentence is wrong, George!'

Mr Somerton thought for a moment.

'These words are clues, George!' he said. 'They are clues about Abbot Thomas' treasure! They will tell us about the hiding-place!'

'Yes, sir! You're right,' said George. '"Gold is hidden in this place." These words are about Abbot Thomas' gold coins. But – "There are seven eyes on one stone." What is the meaning of these words, sir? Are the coins hidden near that stone? We must find the stone. We must find the seven eyes!'

'Yes! We must find them, George,' said Mr Somerton. 'And what is the meaning of St John's clue. Where is the writing on the cloaks?'

'I don't know the answers, George,' said the archeologist. 'But now I will draw these windows.'

An hour passed. Mr Somerton drew pictures of the three figures on the windows. And then he drew some larger pictures – he drew their hands and their faces. Next, he wrote down the words from their books.

The archeologist worked quietly and George looked carefully at the windows. At last, Mr Somerton had finished his drawings. George spoke to him.

'Sir,' he said. 'These windows are beautiful. How did the artist make them?'

Mr Somerton explained. 'There are many small pieces of glass in each window,' he said. 'First, the artist painted all the pieces of glass. Then he heated the pieces of glass over a fire. Now the paint cannot come off the glass. Finally, the artist joined all the pieces of painted glass. He joined them together with pieces of soft metal.'

'Sir,' said George. 'Look at the black paint at the bottom of Zechariah's cloak. The paint is coming off the glass! The artist put the other paint on the glass and he heated it. Then another person put this black paint on the glass. But he did not heat the glass again.'

Mr Somerton looked carefully at the edge of the cloak.

Some of the black paint had come off the glass. The

archeologist saw some blue letters.

'You are right, George,' he said. 'Yes, you are right. There is some writing under the black paint!'

'Some writing, sir?' said George.

'Yes, the words on St John's book are about this writing,' said Mr Somerton. 'St John's clue is, "There is writing on their cloaks. Nobody knows about it." Now I understand.'

'There is writing under the black paint on Zechariah's cloak,' Mr Somerton said. 'Is there writing under the black paint on the other cloaks too?'

'George, please find a ladder,' Mr Somerton said. 'I am going to talk to Lord Dunstan.'

———

A few minutes later, Mr Somerton was talking to Lord Dunstan. The archeologist told him about the writing on the windows.

'I want to remove all the black paint from the three windows,' Mr Somerton said. 'I want to read the blue writing under the black paint.'

'Yes, Somerton,' said Lord Dunstan. 'Remove the black paint. The blue writing will be interesting.'

Mr Somerton returned to the Great Hall. George had found a ladder. He had put it under Job's window.

The archeologist took a small knife from his pocket. He climbed the ladder. He started to remove the black paint from the bottom of Job's cloak.

Two hours later, Mr Somerton had finished his work. He had removed all the black paint from the three windows.

Each of the three figures was wearing a yellow cloak with an inscription – a group of letters – at the bottom. All the letters were blue.

On Job's robe, the inscription was –

ITTASHTHROOMTUATSLSEHWIAGH
KVAEPVHREBIPDBUDDTOEANIGMJU
QYATZRRCDCEIAXASPNJUIRLNEDTB

On St John's robe, the inscription was –

IHNRETTWFHEISLSJLTATBIHBVENEGY
NUTFALERNBDTGIGHAOTNUOIOSSAQ
SNDLTDEGIEOAPNLIDJNCLGPOWIAIN

41

And on Zechariah's robe, the inscription was –

ATYSHADTRNHMEEIGTNPRTTEHO
AEDSAWUEPRLAEGLDNFOEXNNAO
RDTTYWTHAEPKARECBHBDIOSM

Mr Somerton looked at the inscriptions. He could not read any words. The inscriptions did not have a meaning.

'This is a code – there is a secret message here,' the archeologist said. 'The inscriptions are in a code. I must find the rules of the code and I must replace each letter with a different letter. Then the inscriptions will have a meaning.'

Mr Somerton wrote down the three inscriptions very carefully. He wrote them on a large piece of paper. First, he wrote down Job's inscription. Then, he wrote down St John's inscription. Finally, he wrote down Zechariah's inscription.

'Are there three messages or is there one message?' he asked himself.

He thought for a moment.

'There is one message!' he said.

He joined the three inscriptions together. He wrote all the letters on a new piece of paper.

'Now we will go home, George,' Mr Somerton said. 'Tomorrow, I will learn about codes.'

4

The Code

Early the next morning, Mr Somerton sat in his library. He looked at the letters of the three inscriptions on his large piece of paper. There were 242 letters on the paper.

```
I T T A S H T H R O O M T U A T S
L S E H W I A G H K V A E P V H
R E B I P D B U D D T O E A N I G
M J U Q Y A T Z R R C D C E I A X
A S P N J U I R L N E D T B I H N R
E T T W F H E I S L S J L T A T B I
H B V E N E G Y N U T F A L E R
N B D T G I G H A O T N U O I O S
S A Q S N D L T D E G I E O A P N
L I D J N C L G P O W I A I N A T Y
S H A D T R N H M E E I G T N P R
T T E H O A E D S A W U E P R L A
E G L D N F O E X N N A O R D T T
Y W T H A E P K A R E C B H B D I
O S M
```

Mr Somerton looked at the letters for a long time. They did not have a meaning. They did not make any English words.

The archeologist took a book from a bookshelf. The

book was about old codes. He read about many of the codes. Then he wrote different letters underneath the letters of the inscription.

All day, Mr Somerton worked. He tried to use one code. He did not find a message. Then he tried to use another code.

By five o'clock, he had used all the codes in his book. But the writer of the message had not used any of these codes.

———

The next morning, Mr Somerton sat in his library again. He thought about the problem.

'Which letter is written most often in this inscription?' he asked himself. 'Which is the most common letter in the inscription?'

The archeologist started to count the letters. After fifteen minutes, he had finished counting. The letter T was the most common letter in the inscription. It was written twenty-four times.

'The letter E is the most common letter in English words,' Mr Somerton thought. 'Is E the most common letter in this message? There are twenty-six letters in the alphabet. E is the fifth letter of the alphabet. T is the twentieth letter of the alphabet. Was every letter of the message changed by fifteen letters. Was the inscription made in this way?'

Mr Somerton wrote the alphabet on a piece of paper. He wrote the alphabet from A to Z. Over these letters, he wrote the alphabet again. But this time, he started with P, the sixteenth letter. He wrote P over A and Q over B. He wrote R over C and S over D. He wrote all the letters of the alphabet in this way.

P	Q	R	S	T	U	V	W
A	B	C	D	E	F	G	H
X	Y	Z	A	B	C	D	E
I	J	K	L	M	N	O	P
F	G	H	I	J	K	L	M
Q	R	S	T	U	V	W	X
N	O						
Y	Z						

Mr Somerton took another piece of paper. He looked at the first four letters of the inscription – ITTA. He wrote down TEEL. Then he looked at the next four letters of the inscription – SHTH. He wrote down DSES.

'TEELDSES! No, that isn't correct,' he said to himself. 'There are no English words there. I must try another code.'

The archeologist worked all that day. And he worked all the next day too. But he did not find the correct code. He did not read the message.

On Thursday morning, Mr Somerton was very tired.

'I'll never find the correct code,' he thought. 'And I'll never find Abbot Thomas' treasure.'

The archeologist looked again at his drawings of the three windows.

'Are there any other clues?' he asked himself.

He picked up his picture of the right hands of the three people in the windows. He looked at the three hands very carefully.

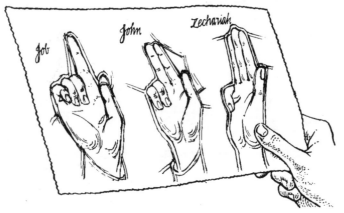

In the first window, Job was holding up his right hand. And one of his fingers was raised. In the second window, St John was holding up his right hand too. But two of his fingers were raised. And in the third window, three of Zechariah's fingers were raised.

'Is ONE-TWO-THREE a part of the code?' Mr Somerton asked himself. 'Abbot Thomas said, "Job, John and Zechariah will tell you!" Are Job, John and Zechariah telling me about the treasure? Are they telling me about it with their fingers?'

Mr Somerton looked again at the inscription. He started to work again.

'I'll underline the first letter,' he said to himself.

He drew a line under the first letter, I.

'Then I'll leave *one* letter. Then I'll underline the next letter and I'll leave *two* letters. Then I'll underline the next letter and I'll leave *three* letters. Then I'll underline the next letter and I'll leave *one* letter again. And then two and then three. And then one again.'

Soon, the archeologist had underlined 81 letters.

I T <u>I</u> A S H T H R O O <u>M</u> T U A T S
L S E <u>H</u> W I A G H K V A E P V H
R E B I P D B U D <u>D</u> T O E A N I G
M J U Q Y A <u>I</u> Z R R C D C E I A X
A S P N J U I R L N E <u>D</u> T B I H N R
E <u>T</u> T W F H E I S L S J L T A T B I
H B V E N E G <u>Y</u> N U <u>I</u> F A L E R
N B D T G I G H A O T N U O I O S
S <u>A</u> Q S N D L T D E G I E O A P N
L I <u>D</u> J N C L G P <u>O</u> W I A I N A T Y
S H A D T R <u>N</u> H M E <u>E</u> I G T N P R
T T E H O A E D S A <u>W</u> U E P R L A
E G L D <u>N</u> F O E X <u>N</u> N A O R D T T
Y W T <u>H</u> A E P K A R E C B H <u>B</u> D I
O S M

47

Then Mr Somerton wrote those letters on another piece of paper. He looked at the letters for a few moments and then he smiled. He put in some spaces and some punctuation.

'This is the beginning of the message,' he said to himself.

> *I, THOMAS, HAVE HIDDEN MY TREASURE IN THIS ABBEY. TEN THOUSAND GOLD COINS ARE IN THE WELL NEAR THE ABBO*

He looked at the piece of paper with the 242 letters from the windows. He had underlined 81 letters. They were the letters in the first part of the message. There were two letters in the inscription after the last underlined letter. These two letters were S and M.

'I must leave these two letters,' thought Mr Somerton. 'And I must go back to the beginning of the inscription. 161 letters are not underlined. I must write out those letters.'

The archeologist wrote the letters on another piece of paper.

'Will these letters – the unused letters – give me the rest of the message?' he asked himself. 'I will try to use the same code.'

Mr Somerton looked carefully at the letters on the paper.

T A S T H R O T U T S L E W I G H
K A P V R E B P B U D T O A I G J
U Q A Z R C D C I X A P N J I L N
D T B H R E T W F E S L J L T T I
H V E N G N U F A L R B D G I G
A T N O I O S Q S D L T E I E A P
N I J N L G P W A I A T Y H D T N
H M E G T P R T E O A D S A U P
R A E G D F O X N N O D T Y W T
A P K R E C H D I S M

The archeologist underlined the first letter, T. Then he left one letter, and he wrote down S.

'Abbots,' he said to himself. 'Yes, that is correct.'
He started underlining again. But soon, he stopped. This was not the correct code for the second part of the message!

Mr Somerton looked at the letters carefully.

After a few minutes, he laughed.

'I understand now!' he said to himself. 'I will underline one letter and leave one letter. Then I will underline the next letter and leave one letter. And I will write down one letter and —.'

'Yes, this is correct code!' he said a minute later. Soon he had underlined 81 letters again.

TASTHROTUTS<u>L</u>EW<u>I</u>GH
KAPVREBPB<u>U</u>DTOAIGJ
UQAZRC<u>D</u>CIXAPNJILN
DTBHRETWFESLJLTTI
HVENGNUFA<u>L</u>RBDGIG
ATNOIOSQ<u>S</u>DLTEIEAP
NIJNLGPWA<u>I</u>ATYHDTN
HMEGTPRTE<u>O</u><u>A</u>DSA<u>U</u>P
RAEGDFOXNNODTYWT
APKRECHDISM

Mr Somerton wrote the underlined letters on a piece of paper. He added some spaces and he added some punctuation. Then he wrote the new part of the message again. He wrote it next to the first part.

Now there were 80 unused letters.

'Is there another code?' Mr Somerton asked himself.

The archeologist tried to use some other codes. But he could not make any more words. After an hour, he stopped working.

'The other 80 letters do not have a meaning,' he said to himself. 'They are not a part of the message. The message is complete. Now I know the secret of Abbot Thomas' treasure. Job, John and Zechariah have told me about it.'

I, THOMAS, HAVE HIDDEN MY TREASURE IN THIS ABBEY. TEN THOUSAND GOLD COINS ARE IN THE WELL NEAR THE ABBOT'S HOUSE. I HAVE PUT A GUARDIAN IN THE WELL. THE GUARDIAN IS SLEEPING WITH THE TREASURE. DO NOT WAKE HIM.

Mr Somerton heard his servant come into the room.

'Look at this, George,' he said.

George looked at the message.

'What is the guardian, sir?' he asked.

'I don't know, George,' Mr Somerton said. 'But Abbot Thomas lived a long time ago. He lived 350 years ago. The guardian is dead now! Put some clothes in our cases, George. We will go to St. Bega's Abbey tomorrow! We will find Abbot Thomas' treasure!'

5

The Well at the Abbey

Early the next morning, Mr Somerton spoke to George.

'We will leave the house in one hour, George,' the archeologist said. 'Please find a large hammer and an iron bar. Also, find a long rope. Put them in my case. Now I am going to visit Mr Gregory. I will return soon.'

Mr Gregory was a clergyman. He worked in the church in the village. He lived near Mr Somerton. Mr Gregory was the archeologist's friend.

Mr Somerton walked quickly to Mr Gregory's house. The clergyman was reading a book in his library.

'I am going away for a few days, Gregory,' said the archeologist. 'Something has happened! I'm very excited! Look at this!'

Mr Somerton showed the old book, *The History of St Bega's Abbey*, to his friend. He told Mr Gregory about the abbey. He told him about Lord Dunstan's window. He told him about the code. And he told the clergyman about the well and the guardian.

'Be careful, Somerton!' said Mr Gregory. 'Please, be very careful!'

———

At nine o'clock, Mr Somerton and his servant started their journey to the town of St Bega's. They arrived there very late in the evening. They went to an inn.

'We will stay here, George,' the archeologist said.

Mr Somerton talked to the owner of the inn. The owner gave a map of St Bega's to the archeologist. He told his visitors about the abbey remains. Then the archeologist and his servant went to their rooms. They both slept well.

On Saturday morning, they woke early. They left the town after breakfast. They took the rope, the iron bar and the hammer with them. And they took the map with them. They walked for half an hour. The hills and the fields and the rivers were very beautiful.

At eleven o'clock, the two men found the remains of the abbey. They found many broken stones and they found small parts of walls.

On some of the stones, there were very old carvings. Mr Somerton looked at the remains. He was happy!

'These stones are the remains of the abbey church, George,' he said. Then he pointed at an old broken

building. 'And that was the abbot's house, over there!'
he said.

The two men walked to the remains of the abbot's
house. They started to walk round it.

Mr Somerton said, 'Now we must find the well.
Then we —.' Suddenly, he stopped talking. In front of
them, was Abbot Thomas' well!

The well-head was very beautiful. It was about three
metres high. It was made of stone. There were carvings
on the stone. The carvings were pictures. They were
cut into the stone.

'There are many stories about wells in the Bible,
George,' the archeologist said. 'Some of these carvings
are pictures from those Bible-stories.'

But Mr Somerton did not look at the carvings carefully. He wanted to go down into the well.

There was an iron wheel in the well-head.

'Long ago, there was a rope over this wheel, George,' Mr Somerton said. 'And there was a bucket at the end of the rope. The monks put the bucket down into the well. The bucket filled with water. Then the monks pulled it up.'

The well had a strong stone wall. The archeologist and his servant looked down into the well. There was water in the well, but it was far below them.

'The water is about six metres below the ground, George,' said Mr Somerton. 'But our rope is ten metres long!'

George pointed into the well. 'Sir,' he said. 'There are stairs in the stone wall. There are stairs down to the water.'

Mr Somerton looked. Yes. There were wide blocks of stone in the wall. There was a block at the level of the ground. There was another block about half a metre below it. Then another, and another. There were blocks down to the water.

'Remember the clues in Lord Dunstan's windows,' said the archeologist. 'Remember Zechariah's book, George. "There are seven eyes on one stone." The seven eyes are down there. And behind the stone is Abbot Thomas' treasure!'

'Somebody is coming, sir!' George said suddenly.

Mr Somerton looked up. He saw some visitors. They were looking at the abbey remains.

'We will go now, George,' said Mr Somerton. 'We will come back tonight. No visitors will be here then. Nobody will see us!'

George hid the rope, the hammer and the iron bar under some stones. Then the two men returned to the town.

Abbot Thomas' Treasure

That night, Mr Somerton spoke to the owner of the inn.

'George and I are going out for two or three hours,' he said. 'It is a beautiful night. The moon is shining brightly. I want to draw some pictures of the abbey remains tonight.'

The archeologist and his servant took some candles from their rooms. Then they left the inn and they walked quickly to the remains. They found their rope, their hammer and their iron bar. Mr Somerton took off his coat and he tied one end of the rope round his body. He put the other end of the rope over the wheel in the well-head. He gave that end of the rope to George.

'I am going to walk down the stone stairs into the well,' he said. 'Hold the end of the rope, George. I will find the treasure in the well. The coins will be in a box or in a bag. I will tie the rope to it. Then you must pull the treasure up out of the well.'

Mr Somerton lit a candle and he took the hammer and the iron bar. He walked down the stone stairs into the well. He walked down, and he looked carefully at the wall of the well. There were twelve stone stairs. Soon the archeologist was standing on the twelfth stair. The water was near his feet.

He looked carefully at the wall near his head. Suddenly, he saw a carving on one of the stones in the wall. Mr Somerton held his candle near the carving. Yes! There was a circle of eyes on the stone! And there were seven eyes!

Mr Somerton looked at the stone again. It was a large stone. He used the hammer and the iron bar. He started to cut the stone out of the wall.

Fifteen minutes later, the archeologist shouted up to his servant.

'George, come down and help me!' he shouted. 'I have found the seven eyes. But they are on a large stone. You must help me. We must take the stone out of the wall. Tie your end of the rope to the well-head. Then come down here.'

A few minutes later, George was standing on the eleventh stair. The two men lifted the stone out of the wall. They put it down next to Mr Somerton's feet.

There was a deep hole in the wall of the well. The stone had covered this hole. And there was a horrible smell! The smell was coming from the hole. It was a very, very old smell! Carefully, the archeologist held up his candle. It's light shone into the hole.

'There is something in here, George,' Mr Somerton said. 'Is it a large leather bag? Is the treasure in it? I will try to get the thing out of the hole.'

Mr Somerton put his arms into the hole. He started to pull the thing towards him. It was wet and cold. The smell was horrible.

Suddenly, the archeologist heard a noise above him.

'Listen, George!' he said. 'What was that? Is there someone at the top of the well?'

The two men listened for a moment. Then they heard the noise again. Somebody was laughing quietly.

'I'll go up to the top of the well, sir,' said George. 'Somebody *is* up there.'

There was a man at the top of the well. George saw him in the moonlight. The man was looking down into the well. And he was laughing. He was a very old man and he was wearing a black cloak. George started to walk up the stone stairs.

Soon, George was near the top of the well. He looked up at the old man's face. And he screamed! There was no skin on the face. The face was white. It had no nose and no eyes. It was the face of a skeleton!

George screamed again and again. Suddenly, the old man disappeared. The servant ran up the last stairs to the well-head. There was nobody at the top of the well! But George heard somebody laughing.

Then George heard Mr Somerton screaming too!

The servant quickly lit a candle and he looked down into the well. Mr Somerton was not standing on the stone stair. He was hanging from the rope. The rope was tied round his body. And he was hanging over the water.

George pulled the rope. He pulled and pulled. Mr Somerton was a heavy man. But soon George had pulled the archeologist out of the well. Mr Somerton's face was pale. He was very, very frightened.

'We must go, George! We must go quickly!' Mr Somerton said. Then his eyes closed. He could not move!

George picked up the archeologist. Very slowly, George carried Mr Somerton back to the inn.

7

The Guardian

Four days later, Mr Gregory arrived in St Bega's. George met the clergyman at the railway station.

'You have come! Thank you, sir,' said George. 'Mr Somerton is ill and he is very frightened. He wants to talk to you.'

'Your letter arrived yesterday, George,' Mr Gregory replied. 'I started my journey yesterday morning. I will talk to Mr Somerton today. Please, take me to the inn now.'

Soon, the two men arrived at the inn and they went to Mr Somerton's room.

Mr Somerton was ill. He was lying on his bed. He was very cold. His face was very pale. His hands were shaking.

'I'm frightened, Gregory,' the archeologist said to his friend. 'Something is trying to find me. I lock my bedroom door every night. But every night, there is something outside the door. Something makes noises outside the door all night. The room becomes very cold. And there is a horrible smell. I have smelt that smell before. I smelt it in the well!'

'What happened in the well, Somerton?' the clergyman asked. 'George told me about your visits to the abbey remains. He told me about the old man. But what happened in the well? Please try to tell me about it.'

'I shall never forget that well,' said the archeologist. 'I saw something in the hole in the wall. I said to George, "Is it a leather bag? Is the treasure in it?" I put my hands on the bag. It was cold and wet.'

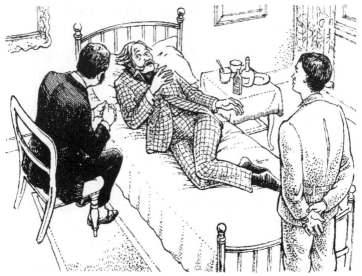

'Then we heard a noise,' Mr Somerton said. 'George climbed up the stone stairs. I put my arms into the hole in the wall. I pulled the thing towards me. But it wasn't a bag. It was alive, Gregory! It was cold and wet and very, very old. It had a horrible smell. But the thing was alive! It put its arms round my neck!'

'I screamed and I fell off the stair,' the archeologist said. 'George pulled me out of the well. The thing was horrible, Gregory – horrible! It was —.'

'It was the guardian,' said the clergyman quietly. 'Abbot Thomas said, "Do not wake him!" But you woke him, Somerton. You woke the guardian.'

'And the old man at the top of the well, sir,' said George. Was he —?'

'Yes, George,' said Mr Gregory. 'The old man was Abbot Thomas.'

'What shall I do, Gregory?' said the archeologist. 'I shall never sleep again. I did not take the treasure, but I woke the guardian. Now it is trying to find me!'

'We must put the stone back into the well,' said Mr Gregory. 'Then nobody will find the treasure. And the guardian will sleep again. George and I will put the stone back today, Somerton.'

'No! No, Gregory!' said the archeologist. 'You will not be safe. You will be in terrible danger!'

'We shall be safe in the day,' said Mr Gregory. 'The guardian wakes at night! It cannot hurt us in the day.'

Mr Gregory spoke to the servant. 'Please come with me, George,' he said. 'We will go to the abbey now.'

———

Two hours later, Mr Gregory and George returned.

'You are safe now, Somerton,' said Mr Gregory. 'We have put the stone back. And I have broken the circle of eyes off the stone. Now, nobody will know about the hiding-place.'

'There was a very strange carving on the well-head,' he said. 'You did not see that carving, Somerton. You saw the carvings of the Bible-stories. But you did not see the carving of a horrible animal! There was an inscription under the carving. The words were, "The guardian is sleeping. Do not wake him."'

Published by Macmillan Heinemann ELT
Between Towns Road, Oxford OX4 3PP
Macmillan Heinemann ELT is an imprint of
Macmillan Publishers Limited
Companies and representatives throughout the world
Heinemann is a registered trademark of Harcourt Education, used under licence.

ISBN 1–405072–32–6
EAN 978–1–405072–32–8

The House in the Picture and Abbot Thomas' Treasure
© N. J. R James 1998, 2002, 2005

These retold versions by F. H. Cornish for Macmillan Readers
First published 1998
Text © Macmillan Publishers Limited 1998, 2002, 2005
Design and illustration © Macmillan Publishers Limited 2002, 2005

This edition first published 2005

Illustrated by Alan Burton
Original cover template design by Jackie Hill
Cover photography by Digital Vision

Printed in Thailand

2009 2008 2007 2006 2005
10 9 8 7 6 5 4 3 2 1